The Biography of Tobacco

Carrie Gleason

Crabtree Publishing Company
www.crabtreebooks.com

Crabtree Publishing Company

www.crabtreebooks.com

Coordinating editor: Ellen Rodger
Editors: Rachel Eagen, Adrianna Morganelli, L. Michelle Nielsen
Production coordinator: Rosie Gowsell
Production assistance: Samara Parent
Art direction: Rob MacGregor
Photo research: Allison Napier

Photo Credits: AP/Wide World Photos: p. 31 (top); Bibliotheque Nationale, Paris, France, Archives Charmet/The Bridgeman Art Library International: p. 4 (bottom left); Dodge Collection, USA/The Bridgeman Art Library International: p. 13 (bottom); Museo Correr, Venice, Italy, Giraudon/The Bridgeman Art Library International: p. 13 (top); Private Collection, The Stapleton Collection/The Bridgeman Art Library International: p. 16; Schlesinger Library, Radcliffe Institute, Harvard University/The Bridgeman Art Library International: p. 17 (top); Bettmann/Corbis: p. 5 (bottom), p. 20, p. 22; Blue Lantern Studio/Corbis: p. 21 (top); Adrian Bradshaw/EPA/epa/Corbis: p. 7 (top); Brooklyn Museum of Art/Corbis: p. 14; Ralph A. Clevenger/Corbis: p. 8 (right); Corbis: p. 11 (top), p. 25 (bottom); Bennett Dean; Eye Ubiquitous/Corbis: title page; Kevin Fleming/Corbis: p. 9; Colin Garratt; Milepost 92/Corbis: p. 25 (top); Handout/EU-Kommission

2004/epa/Corbis: p. 28; Houston/Corbis Sygma: p. 31 (bottom); Catherine Karnow/Corbis: p. 23; Bob Krist/Corbis: p. 27; Andrew Lichtenstein/Corbis: p. 24; Kevin R. Morris/Corbis: p. 8 (left); Carl & Ann Purcell/Corbis: p. 19; Reuters/Corbis: p. 21 (bottom); Reza; Webistan/Corbis: p. 29 (bottom); Royalty-Free/Corbis: p. 5 (top); Paul A. Souders/Corbis: p. 26; Richard Hamilton Smith/Corbis: cover; Susan Steinkamp/Corbis: p, 7 (bottom); The Granger Collection, New York: p. 11 (bottom), p. 17 (bottom), p. 18; Ilyas Dean/The Image Works: p. 30; North Wind/North Wind Picture Archives: p. 10, p. 12, p. 15; Arthur Glauberman/Photo Researchers, Inc.: p. 29. Other images from stock photo Cd.

Cartography: Jim Chernishenko: p. 6

Cover: A farmer examines the leaves of his tobacco plants to make sure that they are healthy and free of pests.

Title page: A woman carries bundles of harvested tobacco leaves.

Contents: The tobacco plant produces flowers while it grows. The flowers are removed through a process called topping.

Library and Archives Canada Cataloguing in Publication

Gleason, Carrie, 1973-
    The biography of tobacco / Carrie Gleason.

(How did that get here?)
Includes index.
ISBN-13: 978-0-7787-2489-6 (bound)
ISBN-10: 0-7787-2489-1 (bound)
ISBN-13: 978-0-7787-2525-1 (pbk.)
ISBN-10: 0-7787-2525-1 (pbk.)

    1. Tobacco--Juvenile literature. I. Title. II. Series.

SB273.G54 2006   j633.7'1   C2006-902468-5

Library of Congress Cataloging-in-Publication Data

Gleason, Carrie, 1973-
    The biography of tobacco / written by Carrie Gleason.
      p. cm. -- (How did that get here?)
    Includes index.
    ISBN-13: 978-0-7787-2489-6 (rlb)
    ISBN-10: 0-7787-2489-1 (rlb)
    ISBN-13: 978-0-7787-2525-1 (pb)
    ISBN-10: 0-7787-2525-1 (pb)
    1. Tobacco--Juvenile literature. 2. Tobacco industry--Juvenile literature. I. Title. II. Series.
SB273.G58 2006
633.7'1--dc22

    2006014373

9462

Published in Canada
Crabtree Publishing
616 Welland Ave.
St. Catharines, ON
L2M 5V6

Published in the United States
Crabtree Publishing
PMB16A
350 Fifth Ave., Suite 3308
New York, NY 10118

Published in the United Kingdom
Crabtree Publishing
White Cross Mills
High Town, Lancaster
LA1 4XS

Published in Australia
Crabtree Publishing
386 Mt. Alexander Rd.
Ascot Vale (Melbourne)
VIC 3032

Contents

A Dangerous Leaf

Tobacco is a plant. It is most familiar to the world as the main ingredient in cigarettes, pipe tobacco, snuff, and chewing tobacco. Tobacco was first used thousands of years ago by Native peoples in South America in religious ceremonies. Today, the most popular use of tobacco is in cigarettes. The worldwide use of tobacco is rising.

▸ *The tobacco plant is believed to be native to South America. Today, it is grown all over the world.*

▾ *The tobacco used by ancient Native peoples of South America was much more powerful than the type of tobacco used today. When taken in large doses it was a hallucinogen. A hallucinogen is a drug that causes people to see things that are not really there.*

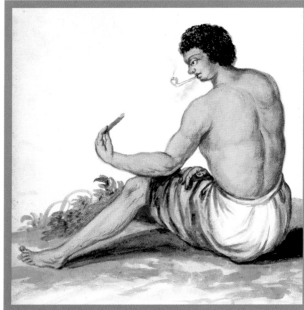

Big Business

Tobacco is grown in more than 125 countries around the world and on over 10 million acres (four million hectares) of farmland. Large, powerful companies control the tobacco trade. The secret of the **tobacco industry's** success is a chemical in tobacco called nicotine. Nicotine is a highly **addictive** substance that keeps smokers hooked and keeps tobacco companies in business.

(below) Chewing tobacco is shredded tobacco leaves. Users put a pinch of it between their cheeks and gums, suck the juices from the tobacco, then spit it out. Famous baseball player Babe Ruth chewed tobacco. He died from throat cancer in 1948.

No Smoking

No Thanks!

The tobacco industry's future lies with turning young people into smokers. Tobacco companies spend billions of dollars each year to advertise to young people so that by the time they are adults, they are addicted to nicotine and continue to buy tobacco products. Until the 1980s, the tobacco companies denied that cigarettes were addictive and that they targeted youth in their advertisements. Today, there are laws in place in the United States, Canada, and other countries to prevent tobacco companies from **marketing** and selling their products to young people.

(above) Tobacco use is increasing, but in many countries the health problems caused by smoking tobacco have made governments pass laws against smoking in public places.

The Tobacco Lands

Tobacco is grown as a cash crop in many countries. A cash crop is a plant crop that is grown for sale, or profit, and not for a farmer's own use. Tobacco plants do not need a specific type of soil or **climate** to grow. One of the few requirements for growing tobacco is that the area has over 100 days a year without frost. Tobacco can grow in soil that is poor, or not fertile enough to grow other crops. Today, the largest producers of tobacco leaf are China, Brazil, India, the United States, Zimbabwe, and Turkey.

Exporters, Importers, and Consumers

The United States is the third largest exporter of tobacco, after Brazil and China. To export something is to sell it to another country. Russia and the United States import, or buy in, the largest amount of tobacco leaf. Most tobacco is used to make cigarettes. The United States exports the most manufactured cigarettes each year, and Japan imports the most. In North America, tobacco use has dropped each year since the 1980s, while in other countries, especially in Asia, tobacco consumption, or use, is rising. People in China consume the most cigarettes, at about 1,643 billion per year.

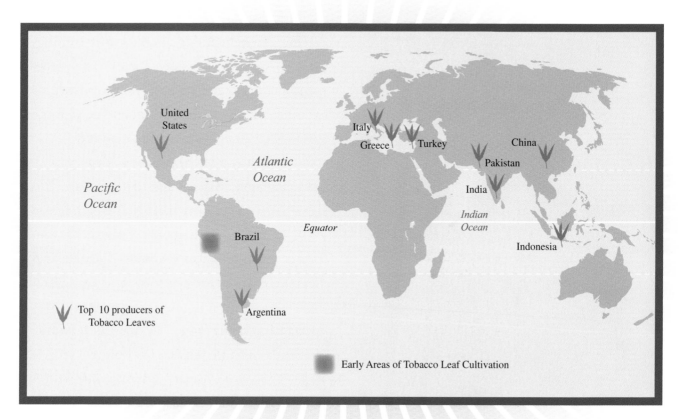

Tobacco first grew wild, and was later cultivated, or grown as a crop, in the Andes Mountains, in what is now Peru. Today, it grows throughout the world.

Tobacco Tax

The import, export, and sale of cigarettes are heavily taxed by governments in every country. Some people argue that high taxes on tobacco products encourage people to quit smoking, and that the money provides revenue, or income, for governments. In some countries, the tax collected from the sale of cigarettes helps the government pay for the cost of treating people with smoking-related diseases. To avoid paying the high taxes, some people smuggle, or secretly carry, cigarettes across borders. Smuggling is a problem in many countries and it is difficult to catch smugglers because their routes constantly change.

A clerk in a cigarette kiosk in Beijing, China. Governments often tax tobacco products because these taxes bring in a lot of income.

Tobacco Quotas

In some countries, governments have quota systems to guarantee farmers a good price for their crop. Under the quota system, only a certain amount of tobacco can be grown per year by each farmer. The quota system also prevents new tobacco farms from starting up. Limiting the amount of tobacco that is available to buyers means that the prices will remain high. The United States recently ended its quota system.

The U.S. was the largest producer of tobacco in the world until the 1960s. U.S. farmers could not compete with cheaper tobacco grown in other countries. In 2005, the U.S. government paid quota-holding farmers to stop growing the crop.

The Tobacco Plant

Tobacco belongs to a family of plants called the Nightshade, or Solanaceae family. Potatoes, tomatoes, and eggplant belong to the same plant family as tobacco. Tobacco is grown and harvested solely for its poisonous leaves.

Nicotine Leaves

Tobacco plants have large, broad leaves. Inside the leaves, the plant stores nicotine. Nicotine is an addictive substance. Scientists do not know why tobacco plants produce nicotine. Some think that the plant produces it as a natural poison to keep harmful insects away. Nicotine does not exist in the seeds of the plant, but forms in the roots a few days after **germination**. Nicotine can be found all through a fully grown tobacco plant, but most is stored in the leaves.

From Seed

Tobacco plants are grown from tiny seeds. The seeds are so small that in just one ounce (28 grams), there are about 300,000 seeds. Those seeds will grow about six acres (two hectares) of tobacco. The seeds are usually planted in greenhouses, where they grow for about two or three months. Then the young plants are transplanted in fields. In the past, farmers planted the seeds in fields, then dug them up and replanted them by hand in another field when they were older. Today, many farmers use machines for transplanting.

◂ *There are many different kinds of tobacco plants. The type most commonly used today is Nicotiana tabacum.*

▸ *Tobacco seedlings make a tasty meal for pests such as caterpillars. Farmers examine their fields regularly for signs of insect infestation.*

The Young Plant

Growing tobacco requires a lot of work. Farmers check their plants almost daily for signs of insects and disease. While the young plants are still in the greenhouses, they are sprayed with pesticides. Pesticides are poisonous chemicals that kill insects and other pests. About three months after being planted in the fields, farm workers pick off the tobacco plants' flowers. This is called "topping." Topping is done so that the plant spends its energy growing bigger leaves instead of flowers. At the same time that topping is done, chemicals are sprayed on the plants to prevent new shoots, called suckers, from growing at the stems. When fully grown, tobacco leaves are about 30 inches (76 centimeters) long.

A tobacco farmer in Tennessee harvests, or cuts, tobacco leaf. Many farmers depend on the income from their small plots of tobacco.

Tobacco's First Users

Tobacco has been cultivated, or grown as a crop, for so long that scientists are unsure of its early history. The first people known to have used tobacco were the Native peoples of South America. They had many ways of taking tobacco, but the earliest was probably by snuffing it, or **inhaling** it through their noses. Other early ways of using tobacco included chewing it, eating it, drinking it, smearing it over bodies, using it in eye drops, and smoking.

Tobacco was used in ancient religious ceremonies by many Native South and North American peoples.

Tobacco and the Spirit World

The tobacco used by ancient Native peoples was more powerful than the tobacco used today. When taken in large doses, it was a hallucinogen. Many Native groups in South, Central, and North America believed that tobacco helped them communicate with gods or spirits. Tobacco was offered as a gift to the gods. In some Native cultures, diseases were thought to be caused when evil spirits tried to steal a person's soul away to another world. By using tobacco, a shaman, or religious leader, was believed to enter into the other world, rescue the spirit, and return the person to good health.

Tobacco as Medicine

Tobacco was also a symbol of cleansing and fertility. In some Native cultures, tobacco was spread over fields before planting. Some South American Native peoples applied tobacco juice to their skin to keep bugs away. Tobacco was also used as a medicine. Packing tobacco leaves around a sore tooth was believed to heal toothaches. It was also applied to skin as a cure for snakebites and used to charm or keep snakes away. Tobacco was part of many tribes' initiation ceremonies, or the point at which a boy is believed to become a man.

Pipes

It is believed that almost all North American Native groups used tobacco. Native North Americans mainly used pipes to smoke their tobacco. Pipes were so important in some cultures that they were buried with dead men to be used in the **afterlife**. Pipes varied in size and decoration depending on their purpose.

▼ *Smaller pipes were sometimes shaped like animals that were believed to be the messengers between the human and spirit worlds.*

(above) Long pipes called **calumets** *were used as peace or friendship pipes by the Sioux people of the American plains. Pipes were smoked at meetings or before going to war. Here, Chief Sitting Bull, at left, who led his people into battle against the United States army, holds a peace pipe with another Native man.*

Tobacco Travels the World

In 1492, explorer Christopher Columbus, sailing for Spain, landed in the Caribbean, believing that he had found a trade route across the Atlantic Ocean to China. He was offered a gift of tobacco from the Taino people of the islands. Columbus and his crew had never seen tobacco before. As more explorers came to the New World, or North, Central, and South America, more Europeans learned of tobacco.

Once tobacco gained a foothold in Europe, religious and government figures lectured about the spiritual dangers of smoking tobacco. It was seen as a vice, or a bad habit.

An Unfavorable Start

European countries, such as Spain and Portugal, set up colonies in Central and South America. **Missionaries**, who came with the colonists to convert the Native peoples to **Christianity,** objected to tobacco use. In 1588, smoking was restricted for the first time in Lima, Peru, when priests were forbidden from smoking or taking snuff before a religious service called mass. In Europe, people were mixed in their reaction to tobacco. Many people associated it with the devil because of the smoke, or with the Native peoples, who they believed to be **uncivilized**.

The Herb that Cures

In the 1550s, tobacco seeds were brought to Spain and Portugal and planted in royal gardens. In 1559, Jean Nicot, the French ambassador, or top representative, in Lisbon, Portugal, learned of tobacco and sent some back to France. He praised its healing powers. Tobacco became known as the "Nicotian Herb." This is where the word nicotine came from. From France, tobacco spread to Italy and what would become the Czech Republic. Many doctors in Europe experimented with tobacco to determine what health effects the strange new plant had.

An early tobacco vendor in Venice, Italy. There was a profitable trade in tobacco, grown on plantations that used slave labor.

Snuff Up The Nose

Snuff was the most common form of tobacco use in Europe before the 1900s. Snuff is finely powdered tobacco that is inhaled through the nose. Snuff was popular among the royalty of France, Spain, and England. Fancy little silver, gold, pewter, or expensive wooden boxes, called snuff boxes, were made to hold the tobacco.

This snuff box was made of gold and decorated with mother-of-pearl and a precious gem called emerald.

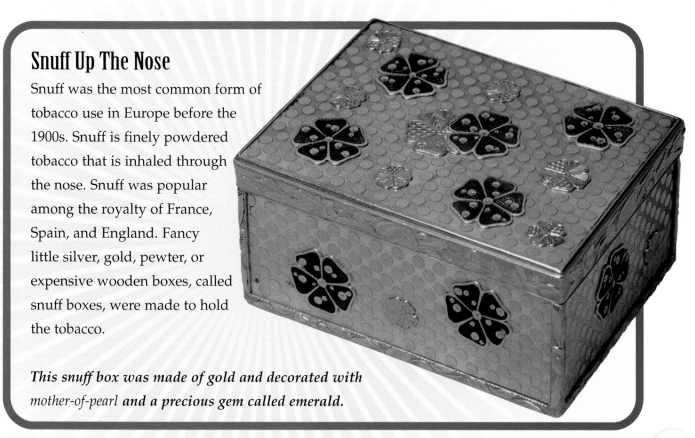

Smoking for Pleasure

Smoking began to be popular in England during a period known today as the Elizabethan era. This was the time in England's history when Queen Elizabeth I ruled. Men gathered to smoke in taverns, or drinking establishments, called "tabagies," throughout England. Under Elizabeth's reign, pirates supported by the government, called privateers, stole from Spanish ships that were returning to Europe from New World **colonies**. Tobacco was one of the most valuable goods that English privateers stole.

▶ *Smoking was introduced to Japan in the late 1500s. Japanese warriors, called* **samurai,** *started smoking clubs and carried fancy silver tobacco pipes. A* **kiseru** *was a long handled wooden pipe that became popular for smoking in Japan.*

Spread of Tobacco

Tobacco is a crop that can be grown almost anywhere. Spanish, Portuguese, and English explorers and traders introduced tobacco cultivation around the world. Spanish traders carried tobacco seeds on trade routes that connected Spain's colonies in the Philippines with Mexico. Along the east coast of Africa, the Portuguese took control of ancient trade routes and introduced tobacco to Arab traders. On Africa's west coast, the Portuguese set up new trade ports and introduced tobacco to the Africans living there.

An early tobacco plantation on the Spanish colony island of Cuba.

Caribbean Tobacco Colonies

Europeans discovered tobacco in the Caribbean islands, but the **monopoly** of the islands as the main supplier of tobacco was short-lived. Tobacco did not become popular in Europe until around 1600. Before that time, the tobacco trade was controlled by the Spanish on their Caribbean colonies, such as in Cuba, where settlers from the Canary Islands, a Spanish colony off the coast of Africa, arrived to establish small tobacco farms. When the European craze for tobacco hit in the 1620s, the English and French established colonies to grow tobacco on islands such as St. Kitts, Barbados, Martinique, and Guadeloupe. Less than ten years later, the Caribbean monopoly of tobacco ended when tobacco started to be exported from England's North American colonies.

15

In Tobacco We Trust

In 1607, England founded its first permanent colony in North America at Jamestown, Virginia. The colony was sponsored by the Virginia Company, a merchant company that hoped to **exploit** the land for its riches and sell those riches back in England. By 1612, the colony was on the verge of collapse. It had made no money and the colonists were dying from disease, starvation, and in fights with Native North Americans. Jamestown colonist John Rolfe learned how to grow, harvest, and cure tobacco from the Native people. In 1613, the first tobacco shipment was sent back to England. By 1624, King James I of England, although against the habit of smoking, took control over the colony's profitable tobacco export.

Tobacco Slavery

Tobacco was the first North American plantation crop. A plantation is a large farm that specializes in growing one main crop. At first, much of the labor needed to grow and harvest the tobacco crop came from indentured servants from Europe. Planters, or plantation owners, paid for the cost of getting the indentured servants to their tobacco plantations and made them work, usually for a set number of years, until the cost was repaid. By the 1680s, few people wanted to work as indentured servants. To meet the demand for workers, planters brought in slaves from the Caribbean, and, later, from Africa.

African slaves working in the tobacco fields.

Centers of Production

The main tobacco growing and manufacturing centers in the United States were Virginia, Maryland, and North Carolina. Small tobacco companies competed with one another to sell pipe tobacco, chewing tobacco, and cigars. In the early 1880s, James Buchanan "Buck" Duke, a tobacco company owner from North Carolina, started making cigarettes using a rolling machine. By 1884, Duke had the machine making more cigarettes than he could sell. To create a demand for his cigarettes, Buck Duke opened a New York factory and covered the city with posters, billboards, and ran newspaper advertisements. He also created cigarette packages that had flashy colors and catchy names to make people want to buy his **brands**. In just five years, Buck Duke's company was selling almost half of all cigarettes sold in the United States.

Buck Duke created a market for rolled cigarettes and went on to build an industry.

Trust and Antitrust

Buck Duke wanted to control the entire cigarette market. In 1889, Duke met with his competitors and created the American Tobacco Company. The American Tobacco Company was a type of business called a trust. In a trust, companies that all sold the same goods joined together under a few leaders, so that there was no competition and prices were kept high. Many other industries were also under the control of trusts, such as the railroads, oil, lumber, and sugar. People who used these products felt that it was unfair market control. Under the United States government's Sherman Antitrust Act of 1890, Duke was forced to end his monopoly in 1911. From Buck Duke's tobacco trust, five independent companies were created that would become known as "Big Tobacco."

◀ *The use of cigarette rolling machines made it possible to manufacture cigarettes quicker.*

Selling Big Tobacco

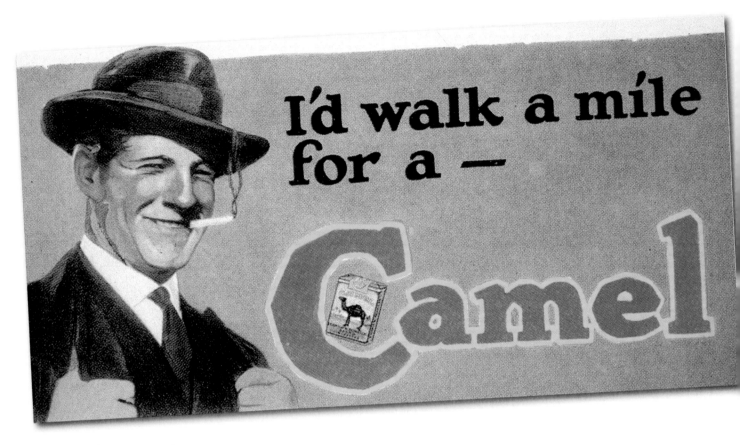

Camel cigarettes began using the catchy slogan "I'd walk a mile for a Camel" when smoking cigarettes was still considered "cool." The brand later introduced a camel mascot known as Joe Cool.

Today, some of the biggest names in the tobacco industry worldwide are Philip Morris, R.J. Reynolds Tobacco Company, British American Tobacco Company, and Imperial Tobacco. Many of these companies are transnational, or multinational companies, which means that they operate in more than one country. Other large tobacco companies around the world are state-owned, such as the China National Tobacco Corporation, which has a monopoly, or sole control over, all of China's tobacco production. These rich and powerful companies are known as "Big Tobacco."

What's in a Name?

Tobacco companies brand their products. Brands are symbols that users identify with a certain product. Brands have slogans, or logos, attached to them, packaging that is easily identifiable, as well as a catchy name. Some early slogans for cigarettes included: "I'd walk a mile for a Camel," "They Satisfy," and "You've Come A Long Way Baby" for a brand aimed at women. The way that brands are presented to the public can often be misleading. Today, tobacco companies spend tens of billions of dollars a year on advertising to promote their brands.

Philip Morris' Marlboro Man

Philip Morris is the world's largest tobacco company. Philip Morris started the company in 1847 in London, England. Morris made his first cigarettes popular by naming them after English universities so that they would appeal to young, rich students. In 1924, the Philip Morris company introduced Marlboro as a brand of cigarettes for women. Around this time, women had begun to become more independent. During World War I and World War II, they did the jobs of men away at war, such as working in factories. As a symbol of their new place in society, women began to smoke in public. Early advertisements for women's cigarettes showed only a woman's hand holding the cigarette because it was still not socially acceptable for women to smoke.

In the 1950s, the image of Marlboro cigarettes changed and the "Marlboro Man" was introduced. Representing strength, bravery, and freedom, the cigarettes appealed to a new audience. Today, Marlboro is the world's most popular cigarette brand.

Cornering the Market

Richard J. Reynolds started his tobacco company in 1875, in Winston, North Carolina. In the company's early days, R.J. Reynolds only made chewing tobacco. In 1913, he created a brand of cigarettes called Camels. Before the cigarettes hit the market, R.J. Reynolds started an advertising campaign to get people excited about the new brand. By World War I (1914-1918), Camels were the most popular brand in the United States and were given to soldiers during the war. In the late 1980s, Camels had a reputation as an "old man's cigarette." To appeal to younger smokers, R.J. Reynolds Tobacco Company introduced a character called Joe Camel in the late 1980s. Joe Camel was a cartoon camel whose image was on merchandise and in advertisements. Anti-smoking groups argued that the Joe Camel character appealed to children. In 1997, R.J. Reynolds got rid of Joe Camel because of the uproar. Since then, R.J. Reynolds Tobacco Company has made a deal with Japan Tobacco, the largest tobacco company in Japan, to sell Camel and other R.J. Reynolds Company brands outside the United States.

Marlboro

SURGEON GENERAL'S WARNING: PREGNANT WOMEN WHO SMOKE RISK FETAL INJURY AND PREMATURE BIRTH.

Ace High

Its a Chesterfield

A Changing View

Until the early 1900s, cigarette smoking was the least popular means of tobacco consumption in North America. Cigarettes were viewed as "sissy" and for "weaklings." Most men chewed tobacco, and most women did not use it at all. During both World War I and World War II, tobacco was given as rations, or supplies, to soldiers. Cigarettes were quick and easy to use on the battlefield, and many soldiers became addicted. Tobacco companies jumped on using images of smoking soldiers in their advertisements. Cigarettes quickly became associated with strength and bravery.

◄ *A smoking fighter pilot improved the image of cigarettes.*

Taking Over the World

The first multinational tobacco company was created when Buck Duke's American Tobacco Company tried to make inroads into the British market in the early 1900s. Thirteen of the largest British tobacco companies united to form Imperial Tobacco to protect their share of the market from American Tobacco. After a short competition between the two companies, a truce was called and a third new company was formed. This new company was called British American Tobacco, or B.A.T. It operated in Asia, Africa, Europe, and Central America.

American Tobacco controlled the market in the United States and Imperial Tobacco controlled the market in the United Kingdom. Today, British American Tobacco is the second largest tobacco company in the world. It owns other tobacco companies in many countries, including Imperial Tobacco Canada Limited, the number one seller of cigarettes in Canada. Cigarette brands are created for each country in which B.A.T. operates to take advantage of different tastes and what might be popular brands. B.A.T. sells over 300 brands of cigarettes worldwide.

State-owned Tobacco

More than 385 million people in China smoke, which makes China the largest market for cigarettes in the world. The China National Tobacco Company is a state monopoly, which means that smaller, privately owned tobacco companies do not exist there. Foreign tobacco companies have only a tiny market share. The China National Tobacco Company produces over 900 different brands. Altadis is a tobacco company that formed when Spain and France merged their state tobacco companies to create one company in 1999. Today, Altadis is the fourth largest tobacco company in the world. In addition to cigarettes, Altadis is the world's largest distributor of cigars.

WILLS'S CIGARETTES

BICYCLES ARE MADE TO CARRY ONE ONLY

Good PR

Public opinion of smoking has changed many times in the past. Tobacco companies give a lot of money away to make the public think good of them. Tobacco companies have donated money to help **civil rights** organizations, the homeless, **literacy** organizations, and arts programs. They have also sponsored, or paid for, sporting events and music concerts. Tobacco companies also donate large amounts of money to political candidates during elections and to political parties to try and influence future laws.

▲ *Cigarette cards were an early form of cigarette marketing and promotion.*

◄ *China is the top cigarette market in the world. Only a small part of that market is for foreign cigarettes but multinationals want more.*

Tobacco on Trial

In 1950, scientific studies of the negative effects of smoking on people's health began to appear in **medical journals** in the United States and England. The studies linked smoking to lung cancer. By this time, almost half of all adults in the United States smoked.

In the Courts

For many years, tobacco companies denied that nicotine was addictive and that smoking caused cancer and other health problems. In the 1960s, smokers and relatives of smokers who had died, began taking tobacco companies to court to sue for the damage smoking had on their health.

The people suing knew that tobacco was addictive and that it harmed their health, even though the tobacco companies refused to admit it. Governments did not want to do anything against tobacco companies because they made a lot of money from the tax on tobacco products. Until 1996, Big Tobacco companies never lost a court case to someone who was suing them for the damage tobacco caused to their health.

In advertisments, tobacco companies tried to say their products were good for people and had no ill effects on their health.

Master Settlement Agreement

In the early 1990s, Mississippi **Attorney General** Michael Moore and lawyer Richard Scruggs brought a lawsuit against Big Tobacco in the United States. They wanted to sue the tobacco companies for some of the costs that the state government had to pay to treat smoking-related illnesses. Other state attorneys general also joined the fight. They accused the tobacco companies of keeping secret research, of altering nicotine levels in tobacco products, and of knowingly addicting children to cigarettes. In 1998, the Master Settlement Agreement was reached. The tobacco companies agreed to pay 46 states $246 billion over the next 25 years. In return, the states would use the money to treat tobacco-related health problems.

Promises, Promises

The Master Settlement Agreement forced tobacco companies to promise not to advertise tobacco products to children. They also agreed to give money to programs to help smokers quit and for tobacco research. They also were not allowed to put their logos, or symbols, on merchandise, in movies, or to sponsor outdoor sporting and cultural events in the United States. The ruling of the case sparked numerous similar cases against tobacco companies in the United States and around the world, including Canada, Australia, and the United Kingdom.

Big Tobacco companies expanded their markets in Asia when the number of smokers decreased in North America.

From Leaf to Cigarette

There are millions of tobacco farms throughout the world. Most tobacco farms are small, family-owned operations. Tobacco is one of the few crops that guarantee a family income when grown on small plots of land. Other tobacco farms are large-scale operations. On these farms, modern machinery is used and workers are hired on permanently to plant and harvest tobacco.

Migrant Mexican farm workers weed a tobacco field in North Carolina.

Tobacco Harvest

Small-scale tobacco farmers hire seasonal workers to help with the tobacco harvest. The leaves are picked a few at a time, starting with those at the bottom. Workers picking the leaves ride on a machine called a harvester. They sit, bending over to pick the ripened leaves. It takes a few weeks to get all of the leaves off the tobacco stalk. In the meantime, some workers become ill from handling the leaves. Some kinds of tobacco are grown in sandy soil, which also makes harvesting a dirty job.

Curing Leaf

After tobacco leaves have been picked, they are cured. Curing is a way of drying out the tobacco, or removing moisture. Curing is done in curing barns. At one time, curing barns were made of wood and heated using wood fires. Harvested tobacco leaves were tied together on a stick and hung upside down in the curing barn, from ceiling to floor. Then the barn was sealed up tight, and the fires were started. This was dangerous because the barns easily caught fire and the fires could spread to the other curing barns. A farmer could lose a whole year's crop and farm buildings. Today, most curing barns are made of metal, so fires are less likely to happen. In warm, sunny climates, tobacco leaves are cured in the sun.

A tobacco worker in Zimbabwe, Africa, prepares leaves for drying.

Child Labor

On family-owned farms around the world, children often help their parents grow and harvest tobacco. In some countries, such as Indonesia and Malawi, whole families work on large tobacco farms. The head of the family is given a quota, or set amount of work that they have to do each day. In order to meet their quotas, children are often brought to work too. In other cases, children are hired directly as workers on large tobacco farms. Children's rights organizations are working to end child labor on these farms.

Child labor was common on tobacco farms in the late 1800s and early 1900s.

Grading and Auctions

After the leaves are cured, they are taken down and bundled in sacks. Each bundle is called a sheet and weighs about 250 pounds (113 kilograms). The farmer takes the tobacco to an auction house. There, the tobacco is inspected and graded by quality. Buyers are hired by tobacco companies to go to the auctions and bid on the leaf. Once purchased, the tobacco is taken to the factories where it is checked for mould or disease. The leaves are moistened and packed into cardboard boxes, where they remain for about one year before being made into cigarettes. Some farmers have a contract, or agreement, with tobacco buyers instead so they do not auction off their leaf, but sell it for a set price.

Cigarette Manufacturing

Cigarettes are made using machines that shred tobacco leaves and then roll the tobacco in thin, white paper. Filters are then added to most types of cigarettes. Cigarette filters are made mostly from a type of plastic that looks like cotton. Their function is to stop bits of tobacco from getting into a smoker's mouth. Nearly two million people work in cigarette manufacturing worldwide. Of all the money that is spent on cigarettes each year by consumers, more of it goes to pay for cigarette filters and packaging than to pay workers.

Migrant workers sort dried leaves at a Canadian farm. Each leaf is sorted by color and grade and then pressed into bales for sale.

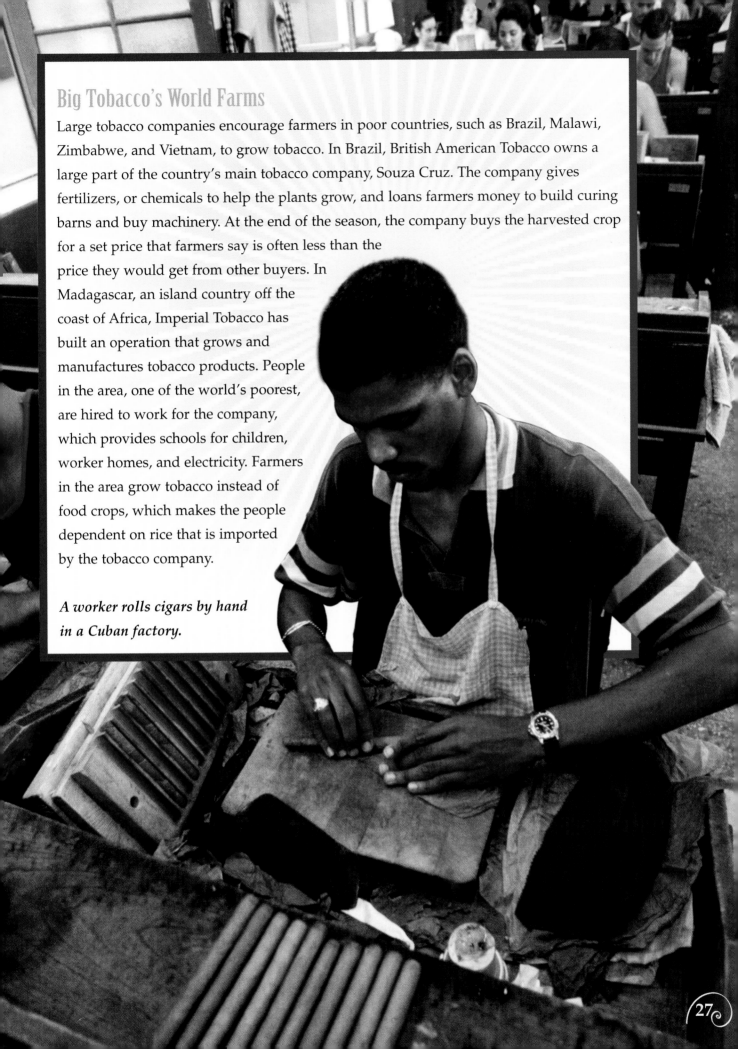

Big Tobacco's World Farms

Large tobacco companies encourage farmers in poor countries, such as Brazil, Malawi, Zimbabwe, and Vietnam, to grow tobacco. In Brazil, British American Tobacco owns a large part of the country's main tobacco company, Souza Cruz. The company gives fertilizers, or chemicals to help the plants grow, and loans farmers money to build curing barns and buy machinery. At the end of the season, the company buys the harvested crop for a set price that farmers say is often less than the price they would get from other buyers. In Madagascar, an island country off the coast of Africa, Imperial Tobacco has built an operation that grows and manufactures tobacco products. People in the area, one of the world's poorest, are hired to work for the company, which provides schools for children, worker homes, and electricity. Farmers in the area grow tobacco instead of food crops, which makes the people dependent on rice that is imported by the tobacco company.

A worker rolls cigars by hand in a Cuban factory.

Tobacco and Health

There is no safe form of tobacco. Whether tobacco is smoked in cigarettes, pipes, or cigars, or snuffed or chewed, all tobacco use has been proven to cause diseases for which there are no cures. Over 3.5 million people die each year from smoking-related causes.

Breaking the Chain

Cigarette smoking has immediate effects on a smoker's body. Nicotine, the addictive substance in tobacco, is a poison that is also used in insecticides. When a smoker takes a drag, or inhales, from a cigarette, nicotine is quickly absorbed into the **bloodstream**. Within seven seconds, nicotine reaches the brain and within twenty seconds it has reached all parts of the body. Nicotine affects the body's central nervous system, which carries messages from the brain to the rest of the body. Nicotine gives smokers a quick boost, or rise in energy level. This boost does not last. Within 30 minutes, smokers start to feel withdrawal symptoms, such as irritability, headache, upset stomach, shaking hands, and depressed mood, and they feel they must smoke again. With every dose of nicotine, tobacco users become more addicted. The only way for users to avoid the unpleasant symptoms of withdrawal is to quit using tobacco for good.

CIGARETTES

Brand

Smoking can cause a slow and painful death

◄ *To prevent people from smoking, anti-smoking campaigns now include images of smoking-related health problems such as this tumor on a man's larynx.*

A User's Body

Tar is the **residue** that is left in a smoker's lungs after smoking. Tar is absorbed by the lungs and causes abnormal cell growth. Cells are units that make up all living things. Abnormal cell growth causes lung cancer. Smoker's lung is the name given to other lung diseases caused by smoking, such as chronic bronchitis, Chronic Obstructive Pulmonary Disease (COPD), and emphysema. People with chronic bronchitis and COPD have swollen, irritated airways, or tubes inside the lungs, which causes them to cough and choke. Emphysema is a lung disease in which tiny air sacs in the lungs are destroyed, making it difficult to breathe. Nonsmoking tobacco users are at risk for throat or mouth cancer. Chewing tobacco can lead to large cancerous growths called tumors to form in the mouth. There are no cures for these diseases, and their victims eventually die.

▲ *A nonsmoker's lungs are red and smooth.*

▶ *A smoker's lungs are dark, rough, and misshapen.*

Youth Smoking

Most smokers start before they are 18 years old. Youth smoking is believed to be caused by peer pressure, easy access to cigarettes, low cigarette prices, and advertising. Low self-image, or not feeling good about yourself, is also a factor. Many teenage smokers do not believe they are addicted to cigarettes. They think that they will be able to quit. By the time they are adults, the negative health effects start to show. The younger a person is who starts to smoke, the greater the chance that they will develop cancer or heart disease.

In some poorer countries, smoking is used to curb hunger. This youngster from Afghanistan is already addicted to cigarettes.

The Future of Tobacco

The number of adult smokers is dropping in North America but is rising in Asian countries. The number of young smokers is also rising. Worldwide, as many as 100,000 young people start smoking every day. An ongoing battle rages between health organizations that try to prevent smoking and tobacco companies, which promote tobacco use. Governments are caught in the middle. Governments make money by taxing cigarettes, but in many countries must also pay the cost of treating tobacco-related illnesses. Tobacco farmers, who depend on the sale of their crop, are also caught in the middle.

Global Epidemic

The World Health Organization (WHO) is an international organization that has launched a campaign against tobacco use. The WHO calls tobacco use a "global **epidemic**," comparing it to a disease that has spread out of control. The WHO has started a public health program to lessen the number of deaths and illnesses caused by tobacco use. The WHO is trying to convince as many countries as it can to sign a **treaty** that will limit tobacco advertising and sponsorship, and increase the number of smoke free areas in member countries.

Pakistani health workers promote the dangers of smoking.

The Future for Tobacco Companies

Today, many large tobacco companies are part of larger, or parent, companies that sell other goods, such as food or alcohol. For example, Philip Morris is part of a company called Altria, which also owns Kraft, Del Monte, Jell-O, Planters Nuts, Lifesavers, and Miller beer. Tobacco companies continue to come up with new ways to promote their tobacco products and new markets to sell them in. In Asia, cigarette companies give away merchandise with their logos on them, sponsor adventure tours, and even hire young women to give cigarettes away for free on the streets. In China, Vietnam, and Thailand, smoking American and European cigarette brands is viewed as "cool."

A Helping Hand

Some tobacco industry experts believe that governments can do a lot more to prevent tobacco use. By raising taxes on cigarettes, they believe that more people will quit smoking as the price per pack increases. Governments can also help farmers switch to growing other crops besides tobacco.

A scientist at East Tennessee State University takes part in a research study on healthy uses for the tobacco plant. The leaf used in cigarettes contains vitamins A and E, among other things.

I miss my lung, Bob.

Anti-smoking advertisments now make fun of popular cigarette brand ads, such as this one that uses the familiar Marlboro Man cowboy image. A lot of money is spent on anti-smoking campaigns, including ones that educate about the effects of secondhand smoke on nonsmokers' health.

Glossary

addictive A substance containing chemicals that causes users to become physically dependent, or feel they have to have it

afterlife The belief that a person lives in another form or place after their Earthly death

attorney general The chief law advisor to a state

bloodstream The blood that flows through the body

brand Names, symbols, and images that represent a certain product

cancer An incurable disease caused by abnormal cell growth

Christianity A religion based on the teachings of Jesus Christ. Christians believe in one God

civil rights Rights that go with citizenship, such as speech, movement, and voting

climate The usual weather of a place

colony A territory under the political control of a distant country

epidemic The outbreak or rapid spread of a disease

exploit To make selfish or unfair use of something or someone

germination Sprouting, or the beginning stages of a plant's growth

inhale To draw smoke into the lungs

literacy The ability to read and write

marketing The selling of a product

medical journals Specialized magazine-like publications that contain articles about health-related topics and scientific discoveries for health professionals, such as doctors, to read

missionaries People who are sent, usually to a foreign country, to preach a religion or way of life

monopoly Having exclusive control over a market or a product

mother-of-pearl The pearly inner part of mollusk shells, such as shellfish and clams. It is used to make buttons and jewelry

residue The remainder of something

tobacco industry The industry that manufactures and sells tobacco products

treaty A formal agreement

uncivilized Primitive or not educated

Index

Printed in the U.S.A.